Marriage

BEFORE & AFTER

T0353248

A. DENNISON LIGHT

TEMPUS

MARRIAGE
—BEFORE AND AFTER

A BOOK FOR THE MARRIED, AND
THOSE ABOUT TO MARRY, WITH
:: :: HEALTH ADVICE. :: ::

BY

The Editor of " Health & Vim."

□ □ □

THREE HUNDREDTH THOUSAND.

□ □ □

[Only Authorised Australian Edition.]

□ □ □

HEALTH & VIM, LTD.,
11 and 12, FINSBURY SQUARE,
LONDON, E.C.

First published by Health & Vim Publishing
This edition published 2008

The History Press
Cirencester Road, Chalford
Stroud, Gloucestershire, GL6 8PE
www.thehistorypress.co.uk

Tempus is an imprint of The History Press

British Library Cataloguing in Publication Data.
A catalogue record for this book is available from the British Library.

ISBN 978 0 7524 4630 1

Typesetting and origination by The History Press
Printed in Great Britain by Ashford Colour Press Ltd, Gosport, Hants.

CONTENTS.

Foreword

With my own forthcoming marriage fast approaching, I – along with almost every other modern bride I expect – have been trawling the Internet for wedding ideas galore. There is indeed a copious amount of inspirational advice covering every aspect of today's wedding; in fact every possibility is explored, from bungee-jumping nuptials to seriously decadent dresses. And yet, despite all this glamorous attention to the special day itself and the much-looked-forward-to honeymoon, there seems little to inform the prospective newlywed of what to expect once the legalities are over and 'real life' has resumed. How is 'the art of a happy and successful home life' achieved? Today many couples already live together, so the shock of finding oneself suddenly co-habiting has already subsided and everyday life together has been successful enough to move on to the next great step: marriage. However, modern life is stressful, and lives are busy, and being a member of a team of two is not always easy when difficult times prevail. Of course, pre-wedding doubts themselves are natural – but how much more comforted would you feel if there was some sage booklet to refer to when facing this new chapter of your life? And lo and behold this book written for the married and those about to be married reached my desk in the nick of time: 'a gleam of light to the perplexed and a guide to all'. Having perused this little gem I now know the ideal age for both a man and a woman to marry (albeit at 31 I am apparently a little 'passed it'), as well as the best time of day for conception and what to do during confinement. In addition there are chapters on homemaking and the inevitable matrimonial friction, and – most tellingly – when not to marry, including 'people who are very thin, very fat, very nervous … for they are freaks' – I will not tell you which of these we are guilty! However, bravely (or foolishly?) ignoring this last, *Marriage: Before & After* is a truly instructive book that will prove invaluable in the years ahead. As the author states: 'Give and take is the golden key to connubial happiness and this is in the realms of the possible where true love abounds.'

Emily Pearce

CHAPTER I.

An acute thinker has said, " The greatest of all human felicities is to be well born "—a blessing enjoyed by few.

See that little child, its inviting face all aglow with golden health! Its gleeful laugh ringing the music of a brave and joyous heart! What a wealth of innocence is there! And yet a few short years and all that attractiveness may be lost and in the place of that tripping fairy will be seen a pale, wasted, weakened elf.

Nothing could be sadder than this appalling waste of human energy and beauty. It is a strange thing when childhood's beauty dies instead of develops. The dreadful child mortality, the wretched suffering condition of hundreds of thousands of poor mites is indeed a blot upon the history of humanity.

Parents are ignorant and the children must suffer.

To say that every child born has the right of health and comfort is only to state the mere truth. But very very rarely indeed does a child come to maturity without having lost, through the ignorance of its parents, many of the noble powers and qualities with which nature endowed him or without a vast amount of needless and cruel suffering. Indeed, it is not too much to say that many a weeping mother to-day tends the tiny grave of the child she unwittingly murdered—murdered through ignorance—slew with soothing syrup and the host of damnable concoctions that violate the sanctity of the nursery room. No, it is not too much to say that thousands of infants are being unwittingly and unwillingly slain in this awful age of domestic ignorance.

If you have been fortunate enough to escape the dreadful ordeal of child life you may be very thankful; but, alas, few streets in our towns and cities are without their squadrons of cripples, and scarcely a village in this fair land of ours but owns its idiot.

But for the purposes of this book we must take it for granted that you are a well developed, well bred, well educated person of correct habits, and that you have arrived at that age when young people are on the look out for life partners and when love romances are such an attraction. You may be " love sick " and wasting away through pining o'er a faithless swain, or you may be head over heels in a happy love affair and fancying yourself suited for ever and a day. In any case this book comes as a gleam of light to the perplexed and as a guide to all, and so with this introduction we may pass on to our next chapter.

CHAPTER II.

At what age ought I to marry? This is an important question that you ought to settle before you allow yourself to fall in love. I know it is customary for young girls of sweet seventeen to imagine themselves like some imprisoned princess in the love tale, and I know that it is likewise customary for boys of 18 and 19 to send surreptitious love missives to the dear girls who sit in the opposite seat in church on Sunday mornings. And so

> *" That monster, custom,*
> *who all sense doth eat,"*

still holds sway, even in the world of love-lore. Young people fancy themselves in love, not because they *are* really desirous of the struggle and joys of married bliss, but because it is customary; and spinsterhood and bachelordom are not so customary as engagements and love knots.

Now marriage should be consummated only between a physiologically perfect man and woman. This physical perfection means that every organ in the human body must be fully matured. A very common fallacy is this that puberty is the age of physical perfection, but this is manifestly wrong, since many of the bones of the body are not completely ossified or full grown until the twenty-fifth year. The bones of the pelvis and leg are not fully formed before the twenty-fifth year. Full investigation goes to prove that in man the period of perfect growth does not arrive until the twenty-eighth or thirtieth year; in woman the period of perfect growth does not arrive until the age of twenty-five.

In man nature is thwarted, by early marriage, in her endeavours to build up a perfect manhood since the life power is directed into wrong channels. In woman, childbearing before the age of maturity is decidedly harmful; for the powers, instead of going to the building up of the body to perfect growth, are directed to the nourishment of the embryonic life, and the result is the birth of an unripe child from an unripe mother. The growth of the mother and child are thus arrested and diminished and old age is greatly accelerated.

A well-known writer says :—" Very early marriages are, in our opinion, a serious evil. Acting under the impulse of headstrong passions, or caprice, or dissatisfaction, young persons too often prematurely rush thoughtlessly and blindly into engagements, which in after life become matters of deep and painful regret. The fancy visions of love's paradise now vanish and the sober realities of life, its cares, its difficulties, and its positive evils, soon lead to discontent, and worse than all, to a growing mutual indifference. Would that such cases were only rare, or only speculative; but the fact is otherwise. We every day see boys and girls at the head of families who want discretion to direct themselves. No wonder that families are ill-governed, children ill-managed, and their affairs ill-directed, when the helm is entrusted to unskilful and inexperienced hands. Is it possible, we would ask, that wives of sixteen or eighteen years of age should possess that discretion, prudence and wisdom so essential to enable them to govern households, rear children, and form their tempers and their principles?"

Another physician of note says:—" Though the laws of nations differ much respecting the age at which marriage is permissible, anatomy and physiology most emphatically assert that persons who have not attained complete physical development have no right to marry. The law of heredity stamps upon the offspring the image of the parent. If the father has not yet attained maturity, in other words, if he is still a boy in mind and body, his boyishness will be indelibly stamped upon his child. This fact undoubtedly accounts for at least a great number of individuals, who, though old in years, exhibit such puerilities of character as to completely negative, in their cases at least, the old adage, 'grey hairs bring wisdom.' A man who wishes to obtain a vigorous and hardy horse would certainly not select one that he knew had been sired by a colt. Boys who contemplate marriage ought to know that the same laws which govern the propagation of other members of the animal kingdom, hold good respecting the propagation of the human species as well, and should consider seriously whether the sons and daughters of a boy-father will be a valuable addition to the human race."

The same writer continues :—" The age at which it is proper for a man to marry is indicated by that at which he attains maturity, which is about twenty-five years. Prior to this age, he is really a boy; his bones have not yet completed their development; the character is not yet completely formed through the development of the mental faculties, and the whole body is immature. Among certain ancient nations marriage was not permitted until some years later than the age named, *and it must be admitted that the people among whom this practice prevailed attained a higher degree of physical development than any nation known to ancient or modern times.*"

We thus clearly see that the best age to marry would be for the woman twenty-five years, for the man twenty-eight to thirty years.

DISPARITY IN AGES.

We frequently hear of cases where a middle-aged man takes to wife a mere girl of eighteen years. Now really there should not be more than two years difference between the ages of the two parties and the man should be the older. All unions between persons of disproportionate ages should be avoided. The power of fecundity ceasing with the one party is often a cause of great immorality, leading the husband to debauchery and the wife to all the excesses of jealousy. The offspring, too, of such ill-assorted unions are always delicate and physically and mentally worthless.

Parsee writes :—" There are great risks run; for in the extreme disparity of age and oftentimes condition—as when the man is rich and the girl is young—Nature avenges herself by spreading scandals, doubts about paternity, and domestic troubles; everything is at variance—age, disposition, character, tastes and amusements. 'What shall I do with him, and what will he do with me?' asked a clever young girl of eighteen, whose parents wished her to marry an old gentleman. With regard to health and vital force, it is easy to see what will become of them in these unequal marriages, where a young and fresh girl is 'flesh of the flesh' of a man used up from age, and perhaps from excesses. Evidently she commits a suicidal act, more or less certain or rapid. On the other hand, experience shows that the elderly man, who thus risks his repose and his powers, speedily finds his health grievously affected."

Dr. Cowan says :—" A man having arrived at thirty years, full grown, perfectly developed, and desirous of marrying, should choose a woman who is not below twenty-four years of age; and a woman at twenty-four, perfectly developed, ripe and lovable, should choose—or perhaps I should say accept—for a helpmeet a man not less than thirty.

" The union of a man and woman at these ages, under right conditions, constitutes the first step towards a perfect marriage."

RELIGION AND MARRIAGE.

I am in no sense a religious fanatic. I believe in the law of religious liberty, but at the same time I feel a word of warning is necessary to those about to marry.

Roman Catholics and Protestants should never intermarry. In the first place the two creeds are so opposed that it is next to impossible for the two to dwell together in harmony, while the tremendous difficulties relating to the children of such parents, merits the entire disapproval of all right thinking and fair-minded men and women. High Church and Low Church people should never intermarry, while the chances of a happy married life are fairly remote in cases where a Dissenter marries a Churchman. Of course, these remarks only apply where the religious feelings of the parties are in activity. A person may be a Churchman only in name and may only have just sufficient religion to attend church when a funeral takes place; in such a case religious strife would be simply *non est*, and in such cases the question of religion would not need to be raised.

THE LAW OF CHOICE.

In many countries marriage is not a matter of choice at all, the parties themselves having no voice in the matter of choosing. The Moors, for example, betroth their children in infancy. The girl may like or dislike the young man about to be her husband, but if he can pay the purchase money, the hatred is looked upon as a womanly freak, her entreaties being of no avail. In Sumatra men buy their wives, and if they are duped they sell or gamble them away for a mere trifle. The Turks are allowed four wives, but neither man or woman has any choice in the matter and they never meet until the marriage takes place.

In civilised countries, however, there is a certain amount of freedom in the matter.

Now about the choice of partners words of warning might easily be multiplied. Briefly, it may be stated that the man or woman should consider matrimony as the most important step in life. Never be guided by feelings alone. "Let reason rule."

Do I *really* want to get married? This should be an oft-repeated question. If you decide affirmatively, then look out for a suitable partner.

A well-known writer has given the

following rules as a guide to those seeking conjugal relations :

" Marry your conjugal mate—your personal duplicate—your approximate equal in development and your like—

" 1. *In age.*
" 2. *In temper.*
" 3. *In intelligence.*
" 4. *In sentiment.*
" 5. *In devotion.*
" 6. *In taste.*
" 7. *In habits.*
" 8. *As to the goal of life.*"

It must be clearly understood that unity of mind is the principle which lies at the base of a perfect marriage and that those who marry should be as like each other as possible.

PHYSICAL ATTRIBUTES IN THE PARTNERS.

The physical attributes of the parties should however be unlike. That is to say, two very tall thin persons should not marry; two very fair persons should not marry; two

very nervous persons should not
marry, else the children may be nervous and anæmic. As a matter of
fact people who are very thin, very
fat, very nervous, ought not to marry
at all, for they are freaks; but it is,
I fear, useless to endeavour to uphold
such a theory and so I say that such
people should marry opposites, a tall
thin person should marry one of
medium build and thus give the
children a chance to be as near normal
as possible. As regards purely physical attributes, opposites should marry;
as regards purely mental and mental-
physical attributes, like should marry
like.

LOVE IN MARRIAGE.

Human love consists of two parts—
the desire for procreation and that
blending of two natures, by some
sublime attraction, into one perfect
whole. Both of these are necessary
to perfect human love, the former the
maternal principle, the latter, mere

affection—the two, the maternal principle and the affection constituting perfect human love.

Love comes to the majority of the human race, and as a rule it comes in youth, *" When the springs of life are fullest."*

The young man or woman has gone along in the full enjoyment of life, when suddenly a huge coiled spring is loosed in his or her breast—love is awakened. The whole of the intellectual forces now centre on the attainment of one object. Every faculty, bodily and mental, is now devoted to achievement of one great aim. This period is one of supreme importance and the decisive nature of the outlet renders it obligatory that very great caution be exercised.

FALSE LOVE.

A few days of wedded experience often sadly dispels the illusions which captivate many. Affairs of mesmerism are not affairs of love. Mesmerism has no part in true marriage. Love a. first sight is a misnomer and is contrary to the law that governs the birth, growth, and perfection of all matter. Tried reciprocity should be the test of love. If a man be found faithful in courting days, marry him; if a woman be found loving, sympathetic and able during courting days, marry her. And here let me say that people who are possessed of real affection for each other will naturally approximate their tastes until a happy and congenial mean has been reached. Give and take is the golden key to connubial happiness and this is in the realms of the possible where true love abounds. The love of your would-be partner should be tested before marriage for a period of not less than two years. Long courtships are to be condemned.

HOW NOT TO BE MISLED.

A man who earnestly desires to be

married should be very careful that his choice be healthy. A woman with a colourless face, flabby muscles, waxy skin, who is hysterical, weak minded, fond of showy clothes, with no ability to work, is not the sort of woman that makes a good mate. A man should look for health, beauty, and natural ability in the person he hopes to marry. All outward indications of an abnormal and unhealthy constitution should be carefully noted. Seek only the woman who is capable of pure love, of right judgment, and of giving birth to vigorous offspring.

WHAT A GREAT PHYSICIAN SAYS.

Dr. Kellogg says :—" Be careful to become well acquainted with the young woman whom your fancy may have chosen before asking her to become your wife.

" Her acquaintance formed at a party, picnic, sociable, or during moonlight walks, or evening parlour

chats, is of very little value in forming
the basis for a proper estimate of
character. A thorough knowledge of
a young lady's character will neces-
sitate a thorough acquaintance with
her conduct at home, her behaviour
towards her parents or brothers and
sisters, her personal habits, etc. Is
she respectful to her parents and
thoughtful of their wishes? Is she
kind and gentle in her behaviour
toward her associates? Does she
respect religion? Is she haughty and
overbearing? Is she simple in her
tastes or does she love pomp, display
and excitement? Has she pure, re-
fined and womanly sentiments or is
she flashy and vulgar? Is she neat
and tidy in personal appearance or
lax and careless? All these are questions the answers to which decide
whether your married life is to be
happy or wretched, peaceful and
enjoyable, or in the highest degree
infelicitous."

WOMEN WHO BREAK HEARTS.

Of all the horrors that threaten the young lover none are fraught with such dreadful consequences as being deceived by a flirt. Do not be unduly jealous, as the imagining that your sweetheart is a flirt is to do her grievous wrong. But do be careful; a flirt is capable of anything mean and should be shunned by any young man. Conscience-seared, she would not scruple at breaking the marriage vow, and if you escape her you should consider yourself a most fortunate individual.

ADVICE TO YOUNG WOMEN.

Although popular parlance has it that the young man chooses the fair lady of his love, yet it is no less a fact that his choice is not absolute, but subject to the young woman's permission. To put it plainly, the young woman chooses the young man in exactly the same sense as we say the young man chooses the young woman. If the woman *won't* then the man *can't*. And so it is necessary that the young lady be very guarded in her choice of husband. Is he a good workman and careful of his money, clothing and reputation? Is he religious or profane? Does he gamble, smoke, drink? Is he a divorced man? Does he treat his mother with kindness and his sisters with gentleness? Is he slovenly? Is he clean? Is he open or mean and close-fisted? These are questions which should decide the choice or rejection of any man who presents himself to you as an object of your love.

Don't marry for money and don't marry merely for a home. Don't be in a hurry. You can, in these days of extensive female employment, earn a good living and there is no need for you to rush into marriage. You will only be called an " old maid " by those whose intellectual make up is of a very mean order and whose opinions, therefore, are not worth having.

WHEN NOT TO MARRY.

A well-known physician says :— " Girls, entertain no thoughts of marriage until you be full grown—until you have arrived at the time termed womanhood. Women, choose and accept only such offers of marriage as will tend to make your united existence a perfect unity, as is required for the birth and growth of love and its attendant pleasures. Failing this, *remain single*, doing your life work with an earnest nobleness of purpose, growing in strength, beauty and purity of soul."

CHAPTER III.

AMATIVENESS : ITS USE AND ABUSE.

Amativeness is the procreative instinct. False modesty has surrounded even the legitimate use of this faculty with an unseemly glamour. It has yet to be widely known that the due exercise of this holy function has nothing shameful about it. The shame lies not in its use, but in its abuse. By abuse is meant what is known as masturbation in single persons, illicit intercourse among the unmarried and excessive sexual cohabitation among the married. Now just as the proper use of the functions of procreation bring joy and contentment by the birth of a welcome and healthy offspring, so its abuse is always followed by ill-health, discontent, peevishness, oftentimes the most horrible diseases and very frequently death itself.

SELF-ABUSE OR MASTURBATION.

This unwholesome habit, which is neither more nor less than the result of a depraved body, has claimed and is claiming thousands upon thousands of victims hourly and yet shows no sign of abatement or decrease. It is a loathsome, hideous monster, ever feasting and never satisfied. Self-abuse has been in all ages the root sin of the human race—the sin which has caused more pain, more shame, and more sorrow than all other sins united. It is indeed very doubtful whether the fairest boy or the most winsome girl you ever saw are totally free from the taint of this poison. High and low, strong and weak, rich and poor, children of the peer and offspring of the peasant—all, all are there in that great vast crowd of soiled and sinful souls.

ILLICIT INTERCOURSE OF THE SEXES.

Second only to the degrading habit of self-abuse practised by both sexes is that still more degraded form of licentiousness, known as illicit sexual intercourse. The limits of this vile sin are almost beyond our computation, for in city and town, in village and hamlet, north, south, east and west, this dreadful sin holds sway.

Illicit intercourse is first of all a sin against reason. Our Creator made us reasoning animals and not the slaves of passions and instincts like the brutes, and for a man or woman to brutalise his soul and degrade his body by such lustful intercourse as that must be which takes place between the harlot and the rake is a denial of manhood and an affirmation of degeneracy. If Darwin's theory be right then such are even yet in the animal stage of their evolutionary existence.

Harlotry is a sin against the divinest impulses in the human make-up. Love and chastity, two of the highest heights to which human beings may attain, are very different to the beastly attributes of the prostitute and whoremonger. Love and chastity exalt and ennoble, harlotry debases and demoralises.

Harlotry is crime. But a tolerated crime. The law, indeed, does make a show of effort sometimes, but utterly futile and useless. This crime seems to be winked at by the authorities in our own country and it is high time that the law relating to public prostitution were enforced with something like respectable rigour. It is a scandal that a young man is unable to take a walk alone after dark without being accosted by street women, and the greater part of the scandal lies in the inactivity of the authorities.

What, I ask, are the police doing to stay the advance and to stop the depredations of this class of criminal? I shall continue asking this question with pen, voice and vote until the authorities themselves answer by such activity in dealing with this matter as becomes the police of a Christian land.

MARITAL EXCESS.

Of one thing you may be sure, my young friends, and that is that marriage is by no means 'legalised licentiousness.' It is a holy estate which none can unthinkingly defile. To act in the marriage bed like the beasts that perish is to rob married life of its joy and peace.

Nothing can so easily break up happy married life as an insistence in either party in too frequent indulgence in sexual intercourse.

Moderation in all things. Do not think that you can with impunity abus' the most intricate and delicate strv tures in your bodies. I tell you, you cannot.

Purity means health and peace; impurity discord and disease. Marry for love, not lust. Take a wife, not a mistress. For a husband take a man, not a weakling, one who *is* a man and who will *act* like a man. I have, in my experience as Editor of "Health and Vim," received many letters from married people on this subject, and from these letters I deduce that there are thousands of married persons who treat the sexual function as an appetite.

Let me explain. You are thirsty, you drink. You are tired, you rest. You are hungry, you eat. *You have sexual desire, it must be gratified.* But this does not follow, for sexual desire is not an appetite. It is a function of the body and is *only to be brought into complete action for purposes of procreation.* The end in view is not sexual gratification, but the propagation of the race. We do not desire to appease an appetite, but to exercise a function.

Do you ask me what is excess? I think you can guess what my answer will be. It is this, whenever you indulge in sexual connection, apart from the object of parenthood, you commit excess.

I tell you, my dear reader, perverted appetite or desire is one thing you must beware of. Just as it is possible to whet the appetite by some savoury delicacy so it is possible to abuse sexual desires, apart from those which follow the desire for children and the joy of parenthood. Continence in the married state is not as difficult as many who have preventive pessaries and suppositories to sell would have you believe.

THE USE OF AMATIVENESS.

The procreative organs in man were designed for a special purpose. God creates, man procreates, and man in the legitimate exercise of this holy office is exercising his highest and most wonderful powers. Cease to think of cohabitation as lust and begin to realise that the sexual function is the God-appointed method of peopling the earth. What a sublime weaving of affection and love and joy and passion is in this procreative power. The work of procreation and the welcome of the baby form together one of the most touching experiences possible to conceive of.

Yes, amativeness is as Mr. Stanley ably says, "The Master Passion of Life." It is the magic key to connubial bliss. It is the consummation of the marriage tie. It proves the man and improves the woman, for be a man ever so good, properly controlled, amativeness proves his manhood;

and be a woman ever such a blessing,
a mother hath still greater calls upon
our respect and affection.

I like the words of Milton where
he says :—

"*Our Maker bids increase, who bids*
*   abstain*
But our Destroyer, foe to God and
*   man ?*
Hail wedded love! mysterious law,
*   true source*
Of human offspring, sole pro-
*   priety*
In Paradise, of all things common
*   else*
By thee adulterous lust was driv'n
*   from men*
Among the bestial herds to range;
*   by thee*
Founded in reason, loyal, just, and
*   pure*
Relations dear and all the charities
Of father, son, and brother first were
*   known.*

*Far be it that I should think thee
    sin or blame,*
*Or think thee unbefitting holiest
    place,*
*Perpetual fountain of domestic
    sweets,*
*Whose bed is undefiled and chaste
    pronounced,*
*Present, or past, as saints and
    patriarchs used.*
*Here Love his golden shafts em-
    ploys, here lights*
*His constant lamp, and waves his
    purple wings,*
*Reigns here and revels, not in the
    bought smile*
*Of harlots, loveless, joyless, un-
    endeared*
Casual fruition; nor in court amours,
*Mixed dance, or wanton mask, or
    midnight ball,*
*Or serenade, which the starved lover
    sings*
*To his proud fair, best quited with
    disdain."*

I especially like the line which reads, " By thee adulterous lust was driv'n from men," and onwards. Let us remember that marriage is the remedy of lust and not the cloak of lust. Then when we have fully grasped the divinely ordained mission of the sexes shall we know what the use of amativeness really is.

CHAPTER IV.

SEXUAL PHYSIOLOGY.

I do not purpose being too explicit in my remarks upon this subject, as I feel that it is my duty to avoid satisfying that unwholesome sensual inquisitiveness which prompts so many to read whatever they can upon the matter of sexual physiology.

I have also a conscientious objection to diagrams illustrating the generative organs, as these are quite unnecessary and only serve in many cases a bad end. I am quite safe when I say that married persons will know enough of the sex organs without the aid of illustrations, suitable only for the eyes of students and doctors.

To the average person these diagrams can teach nothing worth knowing.

To most people of both sexes it might be truthfully said, " You know quite sufficient of sexual physiology to enable you to perform the functions of child-rearing; knowledge beyond this is quite unnecessary and in a good number of instances very undesirable."

THE CONCEPTION OF A NEW LIFE.

This is the consummation of wedded life. Wedded life without children is like summer without the sun, like a year without its summer fruits, the eternal consciousness of something missing in the home. It is well known that married people who have no children are among the most miserable creatures on earth. Marital affection and the love of offspring go hand in hand. Where there is no offspring affection between husband and wife very rarely maintains that high degree of excellence so necessary to a happy married life. The sooner after marriage that the baby arrives the better for both parties. The character of the husband and wife, of course, plays a great part in the generation of offspring. A child born in lust will be very different to the offspring of pure love. Parents should be modest and chaste towards each other and indulgence in sexual thoughts and intercourse as rare as possible.

Dr. Cowan says :—" A requisite to the acquirement of an intellectual, religious, beautiful and sunny nature in the life of the offspring is a life of chastity—of strict continence. I do earnestly advise that husbands and wives, in the practice of this Law of Genius and during the period of transmitted influence, observe closely the Law of Continence, and refrain at all times and under all conditions from the sexual act, save and only as it is required to start the New Life on its voyage into life and eternity. Do you know why it is there is so much licentiousness in the world? Do you know why a son, while yet a boy, practises self-abuse? Do you know why a son, before even he has reached manhood, seeks through prostitution and seduction to foul, blot and weaken his soul and body?

" Do you know why it is that a daughter allows her purity to be defiled, and takes so naturally, as many of them do, to a life of prostitution?

" Would you, oh parents! solve these questions? You have but to ask yourselves, ' Did we obey this divine law of continence? Did we, during the season of transmitted influence, refrain from all sexual sin? ' For if you have not done these things, and have exercised at any or all times the licentiousness that is within you, YOU have transmitted the qualities that went to make your boy an Onanist or a sensualist, and your daughter a prostitute, and YOU stand guilty before God for this great wrong done your children."

Those about to marry, and prospective parents should take serious heed of the foregoing. They should remember that on them lies the responsibility in transmitting to their children either good or bad moral and physical qualities and qualifications.

THE PROPER SEASON.

The best time for a child to be born is springtime, when all nature is revelling in the opening out of new life. There is new life everywhere. The flowers are new, the foliage is new, the grass and herbs are new, animal life is new, all things are new. Let your baby enter into life in April or May.

The warm atmosphere, the long days of sunshine, the wealth of life in the earth itself all help the young infant onwards. It can enjoy the fresh air all day long and the little one will grow strong, healthy and bright.

It should be borne in mind that children born at the approach of winter have not so good a chance as those born in the spring time. For one thing the cold air necessitates a good deal of coddling and confinement, and the result is that fresh air being reduced to the minimum the child grows fretful and ailing. Spring babies, like spring flowers, are the best of the whole year. As already advised, let YOUR baby be a spring baby.

THE BEST HOUR FOR CONCEPTION.

We are children of the light. Now although the night time is usually employed, yet it is physiologically the wrong time. The best time is between eleven and twelve in the forenoon, for at this time the bodily power of a healthy man and woman are at their best. Men and women are always weaker at night than in the morning.

and for a child of beauty and health sexual congress should take place at the time just mentioned. It might be pointed out here that just as the *hour* of darkness is wrong so is the *day* of darkness. On a clear, bright day when the sun is shining is the most suitable time for impregnation to take place, needless to say only after much mental preparation, for the least lascivious expression will be repeated in your child. Keep thine own body and mind pure and only then shall thou give birth and life to a pure and healthy and beautiful child.

GESTATION AND GESTATIVE INFLUENCE.

The beginning of pregnancy and gestation opens up a new era in the life of the expectant mother.

Child-bearing and child-rearing is the crown and beauty of womanhood. Most women, indeed, enjoy better health, are more cheerful and buoyant during pregnancy than during the former life of virginity before marriage. Pregnancy brings, however, not joys to all. Some, alas, through ignorance of health laws or perchance through inherited disease, suffer most agonisingly during the whole period of gestation, only to find in death a relief from trouble and pain on the birth of the baby.

It is sad that very few of our young women, aspirants to motherhood, holding in their hands the welfare of the future, yet care so little about the laws of health. It is, nevertheless, a fact that these young women by their individual violation of these simple laws are disastrously affecting not only their own life and health, but the average health of the nation, and it is easily within the realms of the possible that posterity for centuries may be affected by their carelessness.

Physical organisation and mental characteristics are both transmitted from parents to children, and it behoves mothers and would-be mothers to be healthy and health-wise.

Gestative influence or the influence of the mother on the child she is bearing is also a matter of extreme importance. Displays of temper, moroseness, sorrow, pain, anxiety, fast living, sensuality, sexual intercourse, all have an evil effect upon the forming babe. While on the other hand, cheerfulness, love, light, joy, peace, healthy activity, purity of body and mind, and cleanliness in the mother means the same golden attributes in the child.

THE FATHER'S INFLUENCE.

The father has equal responsibility with the mother in this matter of transmission of qualities. Peculiarities of disposition in either parent are quite likely to be passed on and become the inheritance of the child. Do not blame or praise one parent more than another. Both are praiseworthy or liable. If the father be a thief, a gambler, a drunkard, a swearer and a rogue, depend upon it his children will bear traces of these defects, and it is every man's duty toward the child who shall call him father, to be as pure and as clean as his own inherited qualities and his individual efforts can make him.

A wicked, worthless man, a man who is slovenly, debased, groveling, shiftless, one who is a sufferer from nervous diseases or consumption, cannot hope to be the father of good, healthy, happy children. Only the good, the healthy, the industrious, and the wise ought to marry and become fathers. Not wealth makes manhood, but health. And not by health alone, but coupled with virtue shall a man fit himself for the sacred office of fatherhood.

PREGNANCY, THE SIGNS OF.

A woman in good health having her

digestive and other organs properly performing their apportioned functions, and hitherto having been constantly regular in menstruating, will notice as a sort of first intimation of pregnancy, failure in the recurrence of the menses. This is, perhaps, the best sign, though not always a sure one. In weak and sickly women the cessation of the monthly period may be due to other causes than pregnancy.

"Morning sickness." This is not an ever-present sign, but usually occurs about the third or fourth week.

Mammary changes. Increase in the size of the breasts and the appearance of a number of prominent points or pimples are signs of pregnancy.

Secretion of milk. When the breasts begin to enlarge a milky fluid is secreted, but this secretion taken alone is no sign of pregnancy. Derangements in health involving interruption of the menses may result in the enlargement of the breasts and even in the secretion of milk. Enlarged womb and enlargement of the abdomen are not always signs of pregnancy, but may be caused by dropsy, etc.

However, taken all together, with " quickening," when the motions of the child become apparent, the foregoing are the usual signs of pregnancy in healthy women.

HOW TO AVOID TROUBLE.

The vexed question of corsets assumes its most important aspects when the subject of motherhood comes up for discussion.

Eminent medical men have asserted again and again that the traditional boned corset is harmful, and is especially deadly when tightly laced over the delicate vital organs, crushing them almost beyond recognition.

One celebrated physician says that no young man should marry a woman who tight laces. Now, I go one further and say no young man should marry a woman who wears boned corsets.

Corsets or stays are not necessary for support; in fact, it is acknowledged by all that these detestable engines of torture and death are worn in order to give " figure." A wasp waist and a ponderous bust is the popular conception of beauty.

How far this is removed from the beauty of real health my physical culture readers will know.

Now, in order that this book shall give the most practical advice, I have made careful investigations as to suitable corsets, and I have found that the boneless corsets are much to be preferred to all others. The use of such a corset will restore the fragrant bloom of health to the sallow, pallid cheeks of any young woman, and will prove their service has not been in vain when the critical period of child-birth shall arrive.

DISORDERS OF PREGNANCY.

The bearing of children is a natural
process and there is no reason why
the pre-natal growth of the child
should entail any disorder, disease, or
pain in a perfectly healthy woman.
However, the fact is that the majority
of women suffer more or less during
this period. The underlying source of
this is to be found in the nervous
system. The nerves of organic life
with which the uterus is supplied are
never sensitive in a healthy state; it
is only in disease they have pain.
During pregnancy, while the child is
forming in the uterus, a large supply
of nervous power is drawn from the
rest of the system to supply the
deficiency in the diseased or weakened
nerves of the uterus—hence the out-
lying organs of the body suffer.
Nausea and vomiting, fainting, toothache, etc., all arise in a pregnant
person through this cause.

Morning sickness is considered a

sign of pregnancy, but it is no less a disorder. It usually occurs in the morning when the woman sits up. On rising from her bed she will not feel quite as well as usual and will have nausea, followed by retching. Sometimes this will not occur till after breakfast. If the trouble is insistent the woman should eat less and all longings for special things avoided and kept down. Nothing should be eaten between meals and in the morning a glass of cold water should be drunk.

Costiveness is caused partly by the pressure of the enlarged and enlarging womb upon the lower bowel and partly by improper habits and food. Costiveness of itself is bad enough, but is often the cause of many of the other ailments usually attributed to the pregnant state. For instance, it causes headaches, heartburn, palpitation and fainting. The best and most effectual cure for constipation is the hydrostatic douche. Never take salts or any purgatives. Eat plenty of wholesome fruit and good wholemeal bread. Do not use the ordinary enema. Unless used very carefully and by an experienced hand the enema is dangerous. This cannot be said of the hydrostatic douche. By this method of treatment there is no pumping of water into the rectum, but an even " natural " flow.

In passing I may say the douche is now recognised as a splendid remedy for most complaints.

Pruritis or itching. This is caused in many cases through want of cleanliness. The most effective remedy is cold water, applied in the form of vaginal douches and cold wet cloths or ice. Toothache and headache should have attention. Use the douche daily until cured.

Pain in the breasts may be relieved by washing them in cold water. See that the underclothing is clean, as any pressure of dirty clothing upon the nipples will cause irritation and pain.

There are other pains and ailments, more or less painful and severe, but careful attention to the laws of health will do wonders in making the period of gestation one of pleasure and joy.

GENERAL RULES.

Be clean.

Don't over eat.

Take plenty of exercise, brisk walks, etc.

Be cheerful.

Don't consider yourself a semi-invalid; you are not and should not impose upon the affection or kindness of other people.

CHAPTER V.

CONFINEMENT.

For a favourable confinement a woman must have a strong and healthy constitution and perfect formation of the generative organs.

There must also be a normal duration of pregnancy with good health at the time and proper conduct on the part of the mother and those assisting her.

As soon as the expectant mother calculates the time of delivery to be at hand she should send for her midwife, with whom she will have communicated previously, and see that she has all things in readiness. The advice and help of one clean respectable neighbour, not a dozen, should also be asked and obtained; preferably let the friendly neighbour be a mother of the same age and tastes as the pregnant woman.

A gossipy woman and a slattern should be scrupulously avoided, so also must one of doubtful morals.

The birth of a child is a sacred event and all unseemly jokes should be rigorously prohibited.

WHAT THE EXPECTANT MOTHER NEEDS.

The first thing the expectant mother needs is loving attention from the father of her babe. A dutiful and thoughtful and attentive husband increases the joy and strength of a mother-to-be a thousandfold. But no husband should intrude upon that part of the confinement work which is essentially the work of women folk.

I know one man who busied himself doing housework downstairs and left the lying-in room severely alone, excepting for a few minutes when he took the nurse a cup of tea.

Another husband saw that all things were in order and that hot water, etc., was handy, then giving instructions that he was to be called in case of emergency, he went quietly into another bedroom and slept, waking up at seven o'clock a.m. to find himself the father of a little girl.

I know another though who would persist in superintending matters and saying what ought and ought not to be done.

Now of these three men the first was very thoughtful, the second very sensible, and the last very foolish.

The expectant mother should also see that she has in readiness a douche, a pair of scissors, a narrow strong white thread, sponges of various sizes, chemically purified wadding, flannel, olive oil, a washing basin, towels and sheets, a small bath, hot water, soap, baby linen, and linen for herself.

HOW THE MOTHER SHOULD ACT.

First of all the expectant mother should get as much reliable information on the subject as possible, and this information made use of in an intelligent manner will save much trouble and anxiety.

It is not an unknown thing for nurses and doctors to tamper with the work of nature, and very often with most serious results.

I know one woman whose first-born has a most horrible scalp deformation caused, beyond doubt, by the meddlesome doctor's interference. The husband of this woman grimly remarked to me one day, "No more doctors for this house. We always have the old-fashioned midwife now!"

And I do not blame him.

I do not wish to condemn or even speak slightingly of any profession, but here I cannot refrain from saying that I have a well-grounded objection to the presence of doctors and hospital-trained nurses in the lying-in chamber.

The midwife is safer than the doctor. " But," you exclaim, " surely the doctor knows more than the midwife ! "

Exactly so, and here lies the safety of the midwife. The doctor knows and hence is bold. The midwife does not know and hence is careful. The doctor understands what the result of a certain action will be. The midwife, who knows quite enough for her business, is not so well versed and hence is careful and cautious. The doctor's action may not be questioned or examined; the action of the mid-wife, should it cause any harm, must be questioned.

Besides all this there is the question of sex. It is a fact that most women would prefer a person of their own sex to attend them at this period, and who is more suitable for this delicate and loving work of help and comfort than one who is herself a woman and a mother?

But whether a doctor or a midwife be requisitioned the woman should intelligently assert her individuality. Few women, however, are strong enough for this.

Every woman should have become acquainted with the *modus operandi* of parturition so that when the time comes she will know how to act and also will be able to detect any harmful or unlawful act on the part of those in attendance.

THE LYING-IN CHAMBER.

The lying-in chamber should be the pleasantest in the house. The *pleasantest* remember and not necessarily the *best*. It should be roomy, well aired, sunny, easy to get to from the living-rooms and not too near the noise of the street or road.

It is not advisable, however, to shut the patient off from *all* noise or she

F

may become despondent. The rattle of a cart, if it be not too near, the sounds in the living-rooms, if they be not too boisterous, will keep the patient in touch with the things of this world and she will not feel herself entirely cut off from the rest of the family.

There should be no unnecessary furniture in the room, no overloaded mantels and tables that need daily dusting.

The furniture, a few restful pictures, the baby's cradle or cot, and a few nice flowers fresh daily, are all that are needed.

Finally, ventilation is a most necessary precaution. It will help the mother to recuperate and will probably affect the whole life of her baby.

A great number of people have some very hazy notions as to what ventilation really is. Provided the clothing, etc., be clean there should, in a well-aired room, be an entire absence of all close odours or smells and a sense of refreshment should be apparent on entering.

If the room smells close or stuffy you may depend upon it that there is too little fresh air. Open the windows wider and see that the flues are clear. Avoid draughts* of course.

The bed, preferably, should be a two-thirds iron bedstead with spring mattress, and linen or cotton sheets and blankets. The blankets are easier to wash than are quilts. A narrow bed is, of course, more convenient during a confinement.

In preparing the bed a large square of rubber sheeting should be pinned over the mattress. It should be about two yards square and secured at each

---

* I feel somewhat conscience smitten as I write these words. I have never yet known a really healthy person to take cold merely through a draught. The cause of the cold is in the body, not in the draught. I suppose, however, that if I had not said "Avoid draughts," most of my readers would have thought me a fresh air fanatic. Draughts of fresh air are draughts of life—to be avoided and eschewed ! ! ! ! ! !

corner with safety pins. Over this is placed the sheet, which must be well tucked in all round. Over these again a second piece of rubber sheeting, secured as the first, and over this a second sheet.

This is termed a double bed and saves disturbing the patient to change the sheet after delivery.

After the child is born the change in the bed can be easily and quickly made, as all that is necessary is to unpin and draw out the upper sheet and rubber protector and a fresh and clean sheet is left. For coverings, the time of the year, the climate and the weather must be taken into consideration, and warmth without weight should be the rule.

NURSING AND NURSING INFLUENCE.

Needless to say there must be entire abstinence from sexual connection between the husband and the newly-made mother.

Sexual indulgence vitiates the milk-stream and depraves the child.

During the sacred period of nursing, when the mother's blood goes to feed her new-born babe, every care should be taken that neither the health nor the morals of the mother be lowered. As when the expectant mother carried her little one beneath her heart, she and her husband abstained from all carnal thoughts and fleshly indulgence, so now the nursing mother and the father should maintain a strict and holy abstinence from everything that tends to deprave.

Indeed a loving husband will never seek that gratification which he must know his wife will unwillingly give.

Every mother should nurse her own child. The secretion of milk should be encouraged by all the means possible, good food, fresh air, careful exercise and loving watchfulness over her little one.

Where, however, it is impossible for a mother to suckle her baby, every care should be taken to keep all feeding bottles scrupulously clean and only the best milk should be gotten.

Contrary to the usual idea, herd milk is better than the milk of a single cow kept for the purpose.

Cow's milk undiluted is unsuitable for a baby of tender age, and for the guidance of mothers the table on pages 70 and 71 has been compiled.

In order to break baby of the habit of feeding by night a little warm water may be given in her feeding bottle. This will cause the child to sleep and will benefit the stomach. Up to five months old give a teaspoonful of fresh cream in each bottle.

Baby should be fed regularly, though some babies will defy all attempts at regularity. Never waken in order to feed.

HOW TO CLOTHE THE BABY.

Only light warm clothing should be used. Let the colour be white as this easily shows the dirt and thus ensures cleanliness. See that it be not tight, otherwise serious injury may be done. While every care should be taken for ensuring the warmth and comfort of the little one, all attempts at " coddling " must be abandoned if the child is to be hardy and healthy.

But I fear I have somewhat exceeded the scope of this book. I hope shortly to issue a book for mothers in which such subjects will be exhaustively dealt with.

Age of Child.	Interval between in hours.		No. of Feedings 24 hours
	By day.	By night.	
During 1st fortnight	2	3	10
2nd ,,	2	3	10
2nd month	2½	4½	9
3rd ,,	2½	—	8
4th ,,	2½	—	7
5th ,,	3	—	6
6th ,,	3½	—	6
7th ,,	4	—	5
8th ,,	4	—	4
8th-12th	4	—	3

Amount at each Feeding.	Total amount in 24 hours.	Mixture.
Table-spoons.		
4	About 1 pint	Milk 1 part, water 3 parts
5	,, 1¼ ,,	Milk 1 part, water 2 parts
6	,, 1⅓ ,,	Equal parts milk and water
7	,, 1½ ,,	A little more milk than water
8	,, 1½ ,,	,, ,,
10	,, 1¾ ,,	Milk 2 parts, water 1 part
10	,, 1¾ ,,	,, ,,
12	,, 2 ,,	Pure boiled milk
14	,, 2 ,,	,, ,,
—	—	—

CHAPTER VI.

THE LAW OF THE HUSBAND.

THE HUSBAND'S DUTY.

Perhaps the word " duty " is a little ill-sounding in connection with home life. To begin with love and loving service and to finish up with " duty " seems rather unfortunate. Nevertheless it is so. While no one talks of the duty of the lover yet somehow we can all speak of the duty of the husband.

But while we can speak of the duty of the husband few of us can define it. Nearly every case must provide its own precedent. For instance, a manufacturer, a manager, a stone breaker, will be and act entirely different at home. In fact home to the one will be misery to the other. The duty of the one will be altogether different to the other.

The stone breaker will start work say at eight o'clock and finish at five; then follow several hours' happiness with his wife and children. The home garden and home itself calls for his attention.

The manufacturer or the manager is troubled over many things that our friend the stone breaker never dreams of. These two have the worries and responsibilities of perhaps a large concern and hence home to them will be not a place of activity but a place of rest; a place where the day's business may be laid aside, perchance forgotten for a few hours.

Now the home life of the manager and the stone breaker may be entirely different, yet equally happy and useful.

The one may come home and hang pictures, and rearrange rooms, and tend to the garden, and be a regular handy man, while the other comes home fagged in mind and body, absorbed in some brain-racking problem or scheme that only the sight of his sleeping child and the soft kiss of his waiting wife can dispel. He sinks into his chair and who says he does not take an interest in his home? Thousands of people! And yet he loves his home with the passionate love of a husband and a father, but when he comes home he is always tired.

And so we can only go so far as to lay down the general rule that the duty of a husband is to love his wife and child and see that his wife is well provided with means of feeding and clothing her household.

SACRIFICING HOME FOR BUSINESS.

If a man holds a responsible position his business hours are usually long and his home hours very short. So much so, that it often seems as though the man were sacrificing his home for his business. If these long hours are going to help his wife or child in any lasting way and are going to make his own life an assured success, then all is well. But if the long hours are going to lessen his influence at home as the head of a house and are destroying the happy home influences that make his wife rejoice amid the worries of her work, then he must seriously consider curtailing his business hours.

I know a gentleman who has for many years made a practice of staying at his office till 8.30 and nine o'clock night after night. He has a boy over whom his wife has absolutely no control. Ought not this gentleman to shorten his business hours and give a hand at the training of his boy? Decidedly so.

There must be thousands of similar cases, differing only in details. Cases where the husband wantonly injures his home life by leaving his wife alone hour after hour, year in and year out, and he himself is away all day and just comes home to sleep.

Of course, late hours are unavoidable sometimes, and an intelligent woman will always be ready to give up her husband's company in such cases. But the fact is that those men who can nearly always leave business at an early hour are the ones to stay long after all the other hands have left.

Just why they stop no one knows. But they do stop, gloating over accounts, reckoning up the profits on a certain move, doing themselves and nobody else any good, merely satisfying their greed and lust for gold.

GOOD NEIGHBOURS.

No one can fully realise what a blessing good neighbours are until they have had an adventure or two with bad neighbours.

Amid all the varied misunderstandings in life none are worse than those which arise between neighbours.

A quarrel about the cat, or the little girl, or the piano, or the fence, will often make enemies of the best friends.

The most philosophical way of treating many of these trifles is on the " give and take " principle. In life there must be a great deal of " give and take." Perhaps while you are shrieking about the next door people's cat, your neighbours are groaning over the weird noises that come night after night, at the touch of your eldest daughter, from your twenty-five guinea piano.

Or perhaps the woman underneath annoys you by shaking her mats on your washing day, when the lines are laden with newly-washed clothes. Well, perhaps you have just upset a bucket of water and spoilt her ceiling !

But it is seldom that the neighbour

question arises where the woman is diligent indoors and refrains from gossip.

Idle talk and gossip have started more than one row. Once a week is quite often enough to talk to your neighbour. Wish her the time of day when you see her and then go on about your business.

TAMING THE SHREW.

A peevish woman is often made so by her husband. Not in every case, however, is this so; and the man is indeed unfortunate who happens to marry a woman who gets vexed and starts crying on the least provocation.

A woman who makes herself wretched with jealousy and is always suspecting her husband and fancying she has all the complaints and diseases imaginable, needs very careful " taming."

The husband should ask himself, " Was my wife a shrew before marriage?" No. Then he must reason, if he be at all amenable to the ordinary rules of reasoning, he must reason I say on these lines:—My wife has altered *since* our marriage. Somehow married life has made my wife peevish, pettish, spoilt, jealous, despondent. Mrs. Jones is not a shrew. Why should my wife exhibit these traits? Is there anything in our habits of life, in my treatment of her that would cause her to change so radically?

It is easily possible that a little reflection like this will decide the husband on such a line of conduct as will in time " tame the shrew."

CHAPTER VII.

THE LAW OF THE WIFE.

THE WIFE'S DUTY.

Some of my readers will question the legitimacy of my right to deal with the woman's side of the subject of duty; some will go so far as to question not merely my right, but my ability.

My critics would say that as a man I am disqualified from writing on what concerns a woman. I do not think so. At any rate, whatever view of wifely duty may be adopted, the husband is either the victim or the hero, and this is where the man comes in.

I do not say that a man has any right whatever to map out a course of moral laws for his wife, but a man has certainly the right to expound and show what he considers might be reasonably expected of a wife.

OUGHT SHE TO BE OBEDIENT?

To my mind a deal too much fuss has been made from time to time over the obedience that a wife owes her husband. But these quarrellers are fighting over mere words, for it seems to me as though there is no question of obedience at all.

What loving wife would not obey her husband? And I ask, what loving husband would not obey his wife?

Obedience is the outward and visible sign of an inward and spiritual love.

But perhaps obedience is the wrong word to use. Shall we call it a loving sacrifice that the one makes to the other, a token of the *perfect freedom* that exists between those who *love perfectly*!

There is, however, a subject about which I would not be misunderstood.

The obedience that a wife owes her husband does not mean that she is to yield to his morbid passions just whenever he thinks fit to demand.

Every wife should be free enough to be able to say to her husband, " Thus far and no farther; I am a wife, not a married mistress." And every husband should love his wife sufficiently to accede to the requests of his wife.

Very often the gratification of the sexual passions means bitter agony to the poor woman, and he is a brute who will not readily restrain his unnatural desires at the prayer of the woman he loves. We will now go on to consider what is best known under the heading of " marital rights."

MARITAL RIGHTS.

I am aware that this is hardly the chapter my readers will expect to find this subject dealt with, and yet, to me, it is the right place.

The subject is one for women. The woman is the victim and it is for her to decide what course of action she will follow.

To yield for the sake of peace is a mistake. Yielding never did and never will bring peace. The man will weaken, his excesses will tell upon him and he will become quarrelsome, peevish, and irritable; he will think less of his wife than if she stoutly resisted. There would be a storm, 'tis probable, if she opposed his wishes; but better one good row than a lifetime of bickering and quarrels.

There is, too, a way to arouse the man's better nature. Most wives know the way to do this, and I feel sure that a loving appeal repeated, perhaps, a few times will have a most salutary effect. But wives and mothers, *do not give in*! Do not ruin your husband's health and your own health, and do not blight and blast the moral nature of your children by libidinous indulgence.

I would like to quote Dr. Kellogg here. He says :—" Several times have we been approached by husbands whose wives denied them the exercise of their 'marital rights.' What are a man's 'marital rights'? Certainly, no man has a right to treat his wife as a prostitute. The man who considers his wife as simply a means of gratifying his animal propensities is unworthy of a wife. He is worse than a beast, or at least has less sense in this particular than most beasts, for as a rule a male beast will not approach a female who is not in a condition in which she desires sexual congress and is prepared to engage in the act fruitfully. We do not hesitate to say that no man has the right to demand of his wife that she shall minister to his passions simply for his personal gratification. It is no part of a woman's marital obligations to thus minister to and encourage a depraved and artificially stimulated appetite. A woman is sovereign over her own body, married or unmarried; and no man not wholly given over to selfishness and grossness will attempt to invade her rights for his personal gratification."

This same eloquent physician says to the husband :—" Conquer yourself. Subdue your lustful cravings. Repress the animal by the development of the intellectual and spiritual. Fight down and trample under foot the beast that rules you. Rise into a higher sphere. Leave behind and below you the gross and the sensual. Do this and you will become a new man. You will breathe a purer and a better atmosphere. Love will no longer mean lust and sensuality, but will become a purer passion, partaking less of sense and more of that divinity which gave it origin."

This is a hard saying and who can

bear it? All those who are ready to rise to the highest in life and eternity and in whose bosoms there glows one faint spark of true love and true manhood.

MAKING ENDS MEET.

Before concluding this present chapter it may be well to touch on a most important point in the duty of the wife.

No true wife will regard her husband's pecuniary resources as inexhaustible. I am no believer in " allowancing " the wife, but I would not willingly allow any woman to spend beyond a certain limit.

There is nothing hard about this providing the woman is sensible and intelligent.

Rainy days are in store. Therefore it behoves every true wife to spend and save accordingly. There should be no living right up to the last farthing. Always save a little every week or month, as the case may be. If only a few shillings, they are worth two and a half per cent. in the Post Office and will come in handy later on.

If the household allowance is one pound, or if it is three pounds, don't spend quite all of it. There is always one thing you can do without for just once.

Remember, I am not advising starvation or meanness, I am recommending economy and thrift, and it often lies in the woman's power to save a little of what has been mutually agreed to devote to household requirements.

CHAPTER VIII.

SUBJECTS OF WHICH MORE MIGHT BE SAID.

HOME MAKERS *v*. HOUSEKEEPERS.

We are constantly being told that the home life of England is not what it used to be or what it ought to be. I suppose that one of the many reasons for this is the enormous travelling facilities that now prevail.

In the good old days of long families and real homes, railways, electric and steam, had not been invented. The theatre, too, was scarcely thought of by the average man or woman. In those days men sought in their own homes that which to-day they travel to obtain.

Needless to say there were no week-end tickets then, and the home circle was the seat of enjoyment.

What a change has come only those well versed in history can tell. Men travelled then, 'tis true; but on business—to-day we travel for pleasure. The myriad places of amusement and means of enjoyment that have sprung up within the last decade were then unknown, and their amusements and enjoyment uncared for and unwanted. To-day poor nerve-stricken men want " a change," as they call it, a " little variety," and so the home life is sacrificed and the hallowed associations of an old English fireside have almost been forgotten.

An Englishman's home is not now his castle, it is only his lodging and his wife is his housekeeper. Only in after years, when the hoar frost has touched the head and when the step falters, only then, I say, does the home fireside become precious.

Alas, that it should be so.

> *" Mid pleasures and palaces,*
> *Wherever I may roam,*
> *Be it ever so humble,*
> *There's no place like home."*

Husbands, wives, love your homes! Make them beautiful! Guard them well! Cling to them! lest the day come when you see your children leaving you one by one with no love and thought of the place of their birth, the place they *should* call " home."

MATRIMONIAL FRICTION.

No matter how easy husband and wife may rub along together, there will be friction. I suppose friction is quite natural, as it seems most married couples suffer from it.

Such friction generally arises over a mere trifle. Married people seldom quarrel over important business; they confide and confer with each other.

But it is when the bacon is burned, or when the best carpet is made muddy, or the milk upset, or some other little thing that might be laughed off, that friction occurs. One of the parties gets into a bit of a paddy and the other helps it on until there is quite a storm in a teacup, and perhaps it may all be over a teacup, or some such unimportant thing.

Of course you know the advice I am going to give—Don't quarrel. That's all. It looks bad in front of your children and you know what youngsters are. I once heard one boy say in most doleful tones to another, " My daddy do cuss my mammy, awful." Was this your boy?

Then they build houses with such thin walls nowadays and the neighbours (you know what neighbours are) will hear nearly every word that passes between you, especially if you get emphatic and raise your voices.

I tell you it is best for your peace of mind, for your mutual love, for your children, for your neighbours, for your reputation, that you rub along without friction.

CHAPTER IX.

"YOUR BOOK, 'MARRIAGE: BEFORE AND AFTER,' IS A LOT OF CANT AND HYPOCRISY"— so reads a letter from my post bag this morning.

I have no desire whatever to answer the charge in my own words or by my own arguments. In my own mind, of course, I am absolutely convinced of its falsity and of its contrarity to Nature and Law. I shall, therefore, let the following testimonials, received during the past month or so, speak for themselves. They will show the hesitating reader that beside himself there are thousands of noble English speaking men and women who thoroughly endorse the statements I have made. Read these letters carefully, and if you can read between the lines at all, you will see how timely and how useful a book " Marriage : Before and After " is :—

F. C. (Co. Kildare). I have had " Marriage : Before and After," and think it a most instructive book.

———

L. N. (Scotland) writes : I must thank you very much for sending on " Marriage : Before and After " so promptly. I was very much struck with some of the truths therein. I have passed it on to my messmates.

———

C. T. (Lancs.) writes : It is with the greatest of pleasure I write recommending your remarkable book " Marriage : Before and After." It is a *very valuable book*, and ought to be read by every one about to marry.

———

F. M. P. (Surrey) writes : Thank you so much for the excellent little book " Marriage : Before and After " sent with such promptness. Sorry I had not written before, but I wanted to read it first, and I have learned many things I did not know. May God bless you in your grand work of striving to uplift the men and women of our nation who are at present marring instead of making it. May your books be more widely read.

———

L. M. L. (Earlsfield) writes : I received your book " Marriage : Before and After," and am delighted with it. I think it should be read by all women, as there is a store of information in it.

———

F. E. C. (W. Kensington) writes : I received " Marriage : Before and After " this morning, for which I am very much obliged. It is to be hoped that every young man and woman contemplating marriage will read your book and give it careful thought. I appreciate your work very much, and the knowledge that one can gain from it.

———

E. S. (Guernsey). I have just obtained your " Marriage : Before and After," and was much impressed by it. It is just the thing for young people. I am a schoolmaster, and have some idea of the vice that exists among young people.

J. K. (Lincoln). I sent " Marriage : Before and After " to my fiancée, who was very pleased with it, and asks me to thank you for placing such a helpful book within the reach of the public.

Miss E. K. (Preston) writes : I think your book " Marriage : Before and After " is splendid. There is no beating about the bush. All straight-forward and open, nothing that anyone could object to. I have passed it on to many of my friends, and they all praise it.

R. T. (Bury) writes : I really must congratulate you on the excellency of your book " Marriage : Before and After," as it is simply fine. The sub-ject is treated in a most gentle manner, giving all necessary information with-out too much detail. In fact, I have no hesitation about my young lady friend reading it.

Mrs. M. (Norton) writes : After having read your book " Marriage :

H

Before and After," I only wish I had known it before. I think it is splendid throughout.

J. C. (Manchester) writes : Many thanks for your book " Marriage : Before and After." I am delighted with it, and it will be a splendid guide for the future.

J. P. (Delhi, India) writes : The book, " Marriage : Before and After," is a good book, and ought to be read by everyone, whether they contemplate marriage or not.

W. J. M. (Chorley) writes : I like your book " Marriage." It is straight, and I feel sure will do good.

J. B. (Cork) writes : I read your book entitled " Marriage : Before and After," and think it my duty to give my opinion of it. The book would, if it had a world-wide circulation, work wonders. I myself highly appreciate this book, and will endeavour to get my friends, one and all, to order a copy of the same.

The foregoing are a few taken at random from my most recent posts. I may say that I am daily in receipt of such letters as these—letters expressing the greatest approbation of this book and its message, and which surely stamp my critics as a vast minority. These entirely unsolicited testimonials are, of course, a source of great satisfaction to me, and I feel that their publication in this chapter will be pardoned by any who may be inclined to think that such a place is unsuitable for letters of this kind. Some of my statements are extreme, and in such an unnatural world as this may be thought almost erratic. Hence, the ideals which I set forth, and their consequent morality, are received with appreciation by thousands of my countrymen, and should have some weight in your summing up of my expressions.

In conclusion, I beg to offer my advice to all those who think that I may be of service to them.

For the past ten years my post bag has been largely composed of letters from those whose bad habits have led them into the thraldom of ill-health. All these letters are, of course, treated with the strictest confidence, and no one need be nervous, when writing for my advice, in giving me the fullest possible particulars.

It matters not what your complaint may be, if you will write me I can advise you.

Do not, therefore, neglect that little but persistent cold, that periodical bilious attack, that occasional head-ache, or that constant feeling of languor and exhaustion. Neglect no sign of ill-health.

As I have already pointed out in previous chapters, you owe it to your children to be healthy.

THE END.